In the bin

2

Mum tips a bag into the bin.

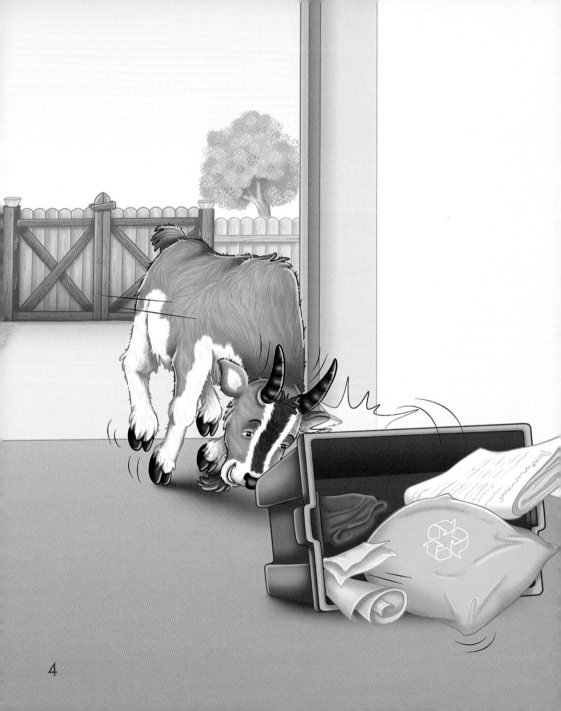

4

Gus runs to the bin and hits it.

6

The bin tips and
the bag rips.

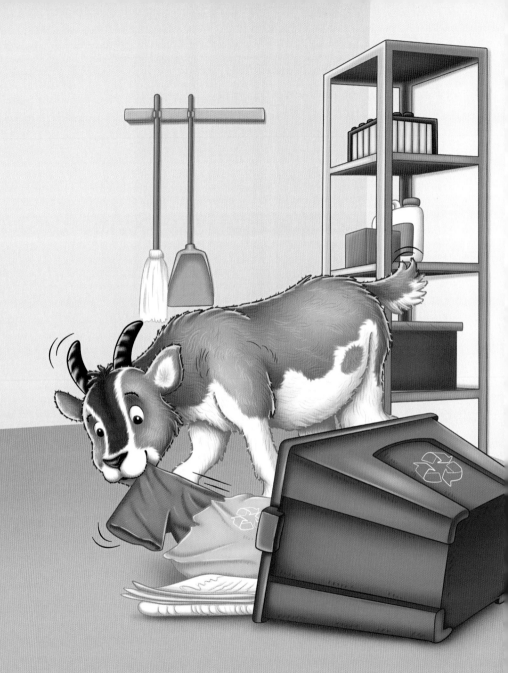

Gus tugs at a red top.

Gus rips the top a bit.

Gus rips the top
a lot.

14

The rags go **in** the bin, Gus!

Before reading

Say the sounds: g o b h e r f u l

Practise blending the sounds: bin Mum tips bag Gus runs hits rips tugs red top bit lot rags

High-frequency words: in a it at **Tricky words:** the into and to go
Vocabulary check: tugs – pulls

Story discussion: What is Mum doing in the cover picture? What might Gus be thinking?

Teaching points: Check that children can say the phonemes /g/ /o/ /b/ /h/ /e/ /r/ /u/ /l/, and that they can identify the grapheme that goes with each phoneme.
Check that children can read longer sentences with appropriate fluency and expression.
Check that children can identify and read the tricky words: the, into, and, to, go.

After reading

Comprehension:
- What happens when Mum leaves the recycling bin?
- What does Gus do to the red top?
- How does Mum feel when she comes back?
- Do you think the mess is Gus's fault? Why, or why not?

Fluency: Speed-read the words again from the inside front cover.